A PLACE WITH THE PIGS

A PLACE WITH THE PIGS

A personal parable

ATHOL FUGARD

faber and faber

LONDON · BOSTON

First published in 1988
by Faber and Faber Limited
3 Queen Square London WCIN 3AU

Photoset by Wilmaset Birkenhead Wirral
Printed in Great Britain by
Cox & Wyman Ltd Reading Berkshire
All rights reserved

This play is fully protected by copyright and application for public
performance should be made to William Morris Agency (UK) Ltd, 147/149
Wardour Street, London W1V 3TB, or to William Morris Agency, Inc., 1350
Avenue of the Americas, New York, NY10019, USA.

British Library Cataloguing in Publication Data

Fugard, Athol
A place with the pigs.
I. Title
822   PR9369.3.F8
ISBN 0-571-15114-0

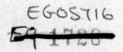

A Place with the Pigs was first performed at the Yale Repertory Theatre, USA. The cast was as follows:

PAVEL Athol Fugard
PRASKOVYA Suzanne Shepherd

Directed by Athol Fugard

The play was subsequently performed at the Market Theatre, Johannesburg, South Africa, with the following cast:

PAVEL Athol Fugard
PRASKOVYA Lida Meiring

Directed by Athol Fugard

The first United Kingdom production was at the Cottesloe Theatre, South Bank, London, on 16 February 1988. The cast was as follows:

PAVEL Jim Broadbent
PRASKOVYA Linda Basset

Directed by Athol Fugard
Designed by Douglas Heap

NOTE

The writing of this play was provoked by the true story of Pavel Navrotsky, a deserter from the Soviet army in the Second World War, who spent forty-one years in hiding in a pigsty.

SCENE ONE

The Anniversary of the Great Victory

A pigsty, in a small village, somewhere in the author's imagination. A dank, unwholesome world. One of the pens has been converted into a primitive living area . . . only bare essentials but all of them obviously already in use for quite a few years. Walls are covered with an attempt to keep track of the passing of time . . . bundles of six strokes with another one across for the seven days of the week, the weeks and necessary odd days circled into months, the months blocked off into years . . . 1944 to 1954. It is a noisy, restless period in the sty – the pigs are waiting to be fed – a cacophony of grunts, squeals and other swinish sounds. PAVEL IVANOVICH NAVROTSKY is in the living area. He is in his mid-thirties, a desperate, haunted-looking individual. He is busy with pencil and paper trying to rehearse a speech.

PAVEL: 'Comrades, Pavel Ivanovich Navrotsky is not dead. He is alive. It is he who stands before you. I beg you, listen to his story and then deal with him as you see fit. Comrades, I also beg you to believe that it is a deeply repentant man who speaks . . .' (*He can hardly hear himself above the noise from the pigs. He speaks louder.*) '. . . that it is a deeply repentant man who speaks these words to you . . .' SHUT UP! (*He grabs a stick and rushes around the sty, lashing out at the pigs.*) Silence, you filthy bastards! I want silence! Silence! Silence!
(*Squeals and then a slight abatement of noise. PAVEL returns to his speech.*)
'Comrades, I also beg you to believe that it is a deeply repentant man who speaks these words to you and who acknowledges the error of his ways . . . (*making a correction*) acknowledges in full his guilt. I, Pavel Ivanovich Navrotsky, ask only that in your judgment of me . . . (*another correction*) ask only that in deciding on my punishment, for I have already judged myself and found myself guilty, I ask only that you temper that punishment

I

with mercy.'

(*The pigs are starting up again.* PAVEL *goes to a door.*)

Praskovya! Praskovya!

(*No reply.*)

Praskovya!

PRASKOVYA: (*A distant voice*) I'm coming . . . I'm coming!

PAVEL: Well, hurry up.

(PRASKOVYA *appears, burdened with buckets of pigswill.*)

PRASKOVYA: I'm coming as fast as I can.

PAVEL: You're late.

PRASKOVYA: I'm not, Pavel.

PAVEL: Don't argue with me, woman! Listen to them. They're going berserk. I can't hear myself think in here.

PRASKOVYA: All right then, I'm late.

PAVEL: Well then, get on with it, Praskovya . . . feed them! You appear to have forgotten that in just a few hours' time I face the severest, the single most decisive test of my entire life.

PRASKOVYA: I know that, Pavel.

PAVEL: I find that hard to believe.

PRASKOVYA: God only gave me two arms and two legs, and I've been working them since I woke up this morning as if I'd been sentenced to hard labour. If you're interested in the truth, Pavel, I'm feeding the pigs an hour earlier than usual so that I will be free to give you all the attention and help I can.

PAVEL: (*Back with his speech*) 'Comrades! Standing before you is a miserable wretch of a man, a despicable, weak creature worthy of nothing but your contempt. In his defence, I say only that if you had witnessed the years of mental anguish, of spiritual torment, which he has inflicted on himself in judgment of himself, then I know, Comrades, that the impulse in your noble and merciful hearts would be: "He has suffered enough. Let him go." For ten years he has been imprisoned by his own conscience in circumstances which would make the most hardened among you wince. Yes, for ten years . . .' (*His voice trails off into silence. Wandering around the sty*) Ten years! Has it really been ten years?

PRASKOVYA: Yes.

PAVEL: Not nine?

PRASKOVYA: No.

PAVEL: Or eleven?

PRASKOVYA: No.

(PAVEL *is counting the years as blocked out on the walls.*)
You've checked it and double-checked it a dozen times
already, Pavel.

PAVEL: Yes . . . ten years, two months and six days to be
precise. There it is! (*Stepping back with pride as an artist
would from his canvas*) Nobody can argue with that, can
they? 'There, Comrades, count it for yourselves . . . every
day of my self-imposed banishment from the human race!'

PRASKOVYA: Sometimes, coming in here to feed you and them,
it feels as if we've been at it for twenty.

PAVEL: Only twenty? Is that your worst? I've had days when it
felt as if I'd been in here a hundred years. Two hundred!
I've already lived through centuries of it. You must
understand, Praskovya, life in here has involved dealing
with two realities, two profound philosophic realities
which have dominated my entire existence, permeated
every corner of my being . . . Pig shit and Time. Just as
my body and every one of its senses has had to deal with
pig shit . . . smelling it, feeling it, tasting it . . . just so
my soul has had to reckon with Time . . . leaden-footed
little seconds, sluggish minutes, reluctant hours, tedious
days, monotonous months and then, only then, the years
crawling past like old tortoises.

PRASKOVYA: You must tell that to the comrades, Pavel.

PAVEL: I intend to.

PRASKOVYA: It sounds very impressive.

PAVEL: (*His speech*) Oh yes, don't worry . . . I intend to draw
a very vivid picture of what I have had to endure in here
right from that very first night.

PRASKOVYA: It was a Sunday night. Your first night in here.

PAVEL: I don't think the actual day is all that important.

PRASKOVYA: Just mentioning it, in case you're interested in the

3

truth. I know it for certain because the storm had kept me from church and I was trying to make up for it before going to bed by saying my prayers a second time, and then a third . . . when I heard the scratching at the door.

(PAVEL's *attention is riveted by her memories of that most decisive night in his life. Encouraged by his attention she continues.*)

At first I thought it was just a poor dog trying to find shelter from the blizzard. But then came the tapping at the window! Oh dear me, I thought, no dog can reach up there, not even on its hind legs! Suppose it's a big black bear! And when I peeped through the curtains . . . Mother of God! . . . that is what I thought I saw, what you looked like . . . all hair and beard and muffled up in your big coat with the snow swirling behind you. But when you tapped again I saw your hand, so I unbolted the door and let you in. But even then it took me some minutes to realize that the pathetic creature I was looking at was you, Pavel. You should have seen yourself.

PAVEL: (*Greedy for still more*) Yes yes yes . . .

PRASKOVYA: Your lips were blue, your fingers frozen stiff. You could hardly hold the mug of soup I tried to get you to drink. I had to feed you like a baby. And then, when your tongue had thawed out enough for your first words . . .

(*She shakes her head in disbelief.*)

PAVEL: Yes yes . . .

PRASKOVYA: You asked for your slippers!

PAVEL: Go on.

PRASKOVYA: And then when I brought them to you, when you saw them, you broke down and started crying. Clutching them to your breast and sobbing . . . Oh, Pavel! Sobbing in a way that nearly broke my heart! . . . You got up, staggered out of the house and collapsed in here.

(PAVEL *fetches a small bundle which has been carefully hidden away somewhere in the living area. He sits down at the table and, after wiping his hands clean on his shirt, reverently unwraps it. He produces a pair of slippers.*)

PAVEL: Oh, dear God! Every time I touch them, or just look at

4

them . . . sometimes when I even just think about them
. . . a flood of grief and guilt wrecks my soul as it did that
night ten years ago. Look, Praskovya, look . . . do you
see? . . . little flowers and birds.

PRASKOVYA: The needlework is very fine.

PAVEL: My mother's hands!

PRASKOVYA: And what a clever pair of hands they were. (*Still
admiring the slippers*) And just look at the colours, still so
bright and fresh! You should wear them, Pavel. One day
the rats are going to find them.

PAVEL: Wear them? In here? How can you suggest such a
thing! That would be sacrilege. No, my conscience will
not allow me to wear these until the day when I am once
again a free man. That is my most solemn vow! (*A little
flutter of hope*) And who knows, Praskovya, this could be
that day. Listen . . .
(*In the distance we hear the sound of a brass band . . . the
discordancies of individual instruments being warmed up.*)
The band has arrived! They're getting ready. (*Pause, then
quietly*) During the war, at the front, deserters weren't
even given a trial. Just forced to their knees and then a
bullet in the back of the head. I saw it . . . blood, bright
red blood on the snow. (*Putting his papers in order*) Pray
for me, Praskovya.

PRASKOVYA: I already have.

PAVEL: Then pray again . . . pray harder! Bully God with your
prayers. I don't just deserve mercy, I've earned it!

PRASKOVYA: I will be down on my knees, Pavel, praying
harder than I have ever prayed in my life from that
moment you walk out that door and leave me. But, for the
last time, Pavel, are you quite sure you are doing the right
thing?

PAVEL: Yes yes YES! Let's go over the ceremony once more.

PRASKOVYA: Again?

PAVEL: Yes, a hundred times again, if necessary. For God's
sake, Praskovya, my life is at stake.

PRASKOVYA: Everybody has been told to gather in the village
square at ten o'clock. The ceremony will start with the

5

arrival of the Ex-Soldiers' Brigade, the Young Pioneers and the Collective Fire Brigade. They are going to march through the village along the route taken by our troops on the glorious day of the liberation ten years ago. When everybody has settled down, we will all join in singing the Hymn of the Revolution. This will be followed by words of welcome from the Village Chairman and the reading of a message from the Central Committee in Moscow. Then the singing of the Victory Anthem, which brings us to the grand climax . . . Comrade Secretary Chomski's speech and the unveiling of the monument. After the unveiling, the School Principal will read out the names of the gallant dead, and with each name, the widow, mother or daughter of the departed will step forward and lay her wreath at the foot of the monument . . .

PAVEL: Which is when I will make my move! I will stay hidden at the back of the crowd until the reading of the names, but when they reach mine . . . *I* will step forward and declare myself. 'Comrades, Pavel Ivanovich Navrotsky is not dead. He is alive. It is he who stands here before you. I beg you, listen to his story and then deal with him as you see fit.'

PRASKOVYA: I'm frightened, Pavel.

PAVEL: You're frightened! How do you think I feel? I'm the one who is going to be standing up there with a thousand pairs of eyes staring at me, judging me.

PRASKOVYA: Suppose something goes wrong?

PAVEL: (*Hanging on*) Nothing is going to go wrong.

PRASKOVYA: I think you may have forgotten what this village is like, Pavel. There are going to be some mean and uncharitable souls out there.

PAVEL: We've already had this discussion, Praskovya . . . and we agreed that the ceremony and the music and the speeches will have an elevating influence on their thoughts and feelings . . . They will have been lifted up to a higher plane . . . They will be forgiving . . .

PRASKOVYA: (*Who has her doubts*) Boris Ratnitski forgiving? Or old Arkadina Petrovna? She packed off a husband, two

6

brothers and three sons to the war and not one of them
came back. They say she's got a picture of Hitler
somewhere in her house which she spits on every morning
when she wakes up.

PAVEL: (*A cry of despair*) Praskovya! Praskovya! I am trying to
hold on to what little courage I have left in my bruised
and battered soul. Don't destroy it! Give me support,
woman! (*He calms down.*) There is no other way. This is
my only chance. The alternative *is* madness . . . or
suicide! I mean it, Praskovya. One more day in here, and
I'll cut my throat! (*Steadying himself*) But that is not going
to be necessary, because I have prepared a very moving
and eloquent plea to the comrades. I promise you,
Praskovya, there will not be many dry eyes out there by
the time I am finished. (*The papers for his speech*) Where is
it? . . . Where is it? . . . Yes . . . Listen: '. . . dark nights
of despair from which the next day's dawn brought no
release . . .' And what about this: 'Remorse was the bitter
bread of my soul in its cold, grey and foul-smelling
entombment . . .' Many was the time you yourself said I
could have made a career of the stage if I had wanted to.
Well, Fate has done it. Today I must give the performance
of and for my life. And I am ready for it, Praskovya. (*His
speech.*) When I stand there in front of them in my
uniform, the truth and sincerity of these words will strike
home.

PRASKOVYA: Stand there in your what?

PAVEL: My uniform . . . as Comrade Private Pavel Ivanovich
Navrotsky, first class, of the Sarazhentsy Brigade . . .

PRASKOVYA: Pavel . . .

PAVEL: They won't see me as an enemy . . .

PRASKOVYA: Pavel . . .

PAVEL: . . . to be punished for his desertion and betrayal of
the Cause. Oh no . . .

PRASKOVYA: Pavel!!

(*She finally manages to silence him.*)

I have got your suit, your fine black suit shaken out and
aired and all ready for you.

7

PAVEL: My suit?

PRASKOVYA: Yes. Don't you remember? You got married in it.

PAVEL: Of course I remember it. But I'm going to wear my uniform.

PRASKOVYA: Pavel, please . . .

PAVEL: We haven't got time for pointless arguments, Praskovya. Don't you understand anything! I'm *surrendering*. A soldier does not surrender in the fine black suit he got married in.

PRASKOVYA: Please listen to me, Pavel . . .

PAVEL: No! Why are you making it so hard for me, Praskovya! Do I have to argue with you and fight about everything? I've had enough of it now. Just do as I say. Go and fetch my uniform. Praskovya! Move!

(*A leaden-footed* PRASKOVYA *leaves the sty.*)

(*Washing himself*) Courage, Pavel. Courage! It's nearly over. One way or the other this purgatory is nearly at an end. (*A farewell circuit of the pens.*) Did you hear that my darlings? I'll be leaving you soon. Yes, my little shit-eaters, you'll have to find another victim to torment with your bestiality. So, in memory of the years we have shared in here, Pavel Ivanovich will leave you with one last gesture of his deep, oh so deep and abiding loathing and disgust.

(*He grabs his stick and brutalizes the pigs, striking and prodding them viciously. The exercise affords him considerable satisfaction. An exhausted and happy* PAVEL *retires to his living area.* PRASKOVYA *returns. In terrified silence she hands over to the still manic and panting* PAVEL *a miserable little bundle. He unwraps it. It produces a few moth-eaten remnants of his uniform . . . cap, torn old tunic, one legging, etc. etc.*) What's this?

PRASKOVYA: I tried to tell you.

PAVEL: Praskovya. . . ?

PRASKOVYA: That's it. And you're lucky there is that much left of it. When you gave it to me you said I must burn it, but I thought that was a wasteful thing to do with such a good bundle of rags, because that is all it was . . . so I just

stuffed it away in a corner and whenever I needed one . . .
(*Her voice trails off.*) I never dreamt you would ever need
it again.

PAVEL: (*Stunned disbelief*) Are you telling me that this . . . No!
It can't be. You are not telling me that, are you?

PRASKOVYA: Yes.

PAVEL: Yes, what?

PRASKOVYA: Yes, that *is* what I'm telling you.

PAVEL: That this . . .

PRASKOVYA: . . . is your uniform . . . what is left of it.

PAVEL: But the buttons . . . shiny brass buttons . . . six of
them, all the way down here in the front.

PRASKOVYA: There were no buttons left when you came home
that night.

PAVEL: Are you sure?

PRASKOVYA: Yes.

(*Stunned silence from* PAVEL *as he examines the rags.*)
I'm afraid the mice have had a little nibble as well.
(PAVEL *slips on what is left of his tunic.* PRASKOVYA *shakes
her head. He puts on the cap and salutes.* PRASKOVYA *shakes
her head again.*)
Somebody might laugh.
(PAVEL *is devastated.*)
Take my advice and wear your suit. It's all ready for you.
A clean white shirt. And I've given your black shoes a
really good polish . . . shining like mirrors they are. It
won't make all that much difference surely. So instead of
Private Navrotsky the soldier, they'll see responsible,
sober, law-abiding Comrade Pavel Ivanovich they all
remember so well. It might even work to your advantage.

PAVEL: For God's sake, Praskovya! Didn't you hear me? This
is a military occasion. A deserter does not appear before
his court martial in his wedding suit. 'Why aren't you in
uniform, Private Navrotsky?' 'Comrade Sergeant, my wife
used it to mop the floor, and then the mice and the moths
made a meal of what was left.' That is sure to save me
from the firing squad! (*Doubts begin.*) No . . . no . . . wait
. . . let me think . . . let me think. (*Agitated pacing.*) This

9

calls for very careful thought . . . a reappraisal of the situation in the light of new and unexpected developments. There has got to be a simple solution . . . which we will find, provided we stay calm and don't panic. (*Pause. His nerve is beginning to fail.*) Suppose I'm wrong, Praskovya.

PRASKOVYA: About what?

PAVEL: Them . . . (*A gesture to the world outside.*) Suppose my innocent faith in human nature, my trusting belief in the essential goodness of our comrades' hearts . . . (*Swallows*) . . . is a big, big mistake. That instead of forgiveness and understanding, when they hear my story . . . maybe . . . just maybe . . . they will hate and despise me. See in me and my moment of weakness ten years ago, a reminder of their *own* weaknesses . . . weaknesses they do not wish to confess to or be reminded of. Because you are certainly right about one thing, Praskovya Alexandrovna . . . that is not an assembly of saints out there clearing their throats for the singing of the anthem. Oh, most certainly not. If the truth were known about some of our respectable comrades out there, I wouldn't be the only one pleading for mercy today. My theory about the elevation of their thoughts and feelings on to a higher plane is dependent on there being enough basic humanity left in them to allow that to happen. But as you so perceptively pointed out, Praskovya, knowing some of them, that amounts to asking for a small miracle. (*Hitting his head*) Stupid! Stupid! Stupid! I've been in here so long, I've forgotten what human nature is really like. Compassion and forgiveness? I stand as much chance of getting that from the mob out there as I do from these pigs.

(*The brass band is now in full swing.*)

PRASKOVYA: So what is it going to be, Pavel? They sound just about ready. It's now or never.

(*Pause.*)

Did you hear me, Pavel? It's time to go. Are you still going out there?

PAVEL: (*Very small and very frightened*) I can't. It's no good, Praskovya . . . I just can't. I won't get a fair trial. They won't even give me a hearing. The moment I appear they'll throw themselves on me and tear me apart like a pack of Siberian wolves.

(*He throws away the papers for his speech.*)

PRASKOVYA: So this is the end of it, then.

PAVEL: For me it is. You are the one who must give the performance now.

PRASKOVYA: Me?

PAVEL: Yes. So prepare yourself.

PRASKOVYA: What do you mean?

PAVEL: Your black dress . . . and didn't you say something about flowers? . . . A funeral wreath! When you hear my name . . . weep, Praskovya . . . weep! Because your Pavel is now as good as in his grave.

PRASKOVYA: (*Nervous*) You want me to go out there . . . in front of all those people . . . and pretend you're dead.

PAVEL: Isn't that what you've been doing for the past ten years?

PRASKOVYA: Yes, that's true . . . but not on such a grand scale, Pavel. Widow's weeds and flowers, with a brass band playing!

PAVEL: Are you trying to get out of it?

PRASKOVYA: Yes! NO! If you want me to go out there, Pavel, I'll do it. But I want you to know that I'm as frightened of going out there as you are. You don't seem to realize that I hardly see anybody any more. The only dealings I have with the outside world now is when I take one of the pigs down to the butcher. For the rest, I'm as much a prisoner in the house as you are in here.

PAVEL: You're wasting time, Praskovya. If you're not out there ready to step forward when my name is called, people will get suspicious and start asking questions.

(*She is very reluctant to move.*)

I'm warning you, at this rate you will end up mourning my real death before the day is over.

PRASKOVYA: All right, all right . . . I'm going. But I'm telling you, Pavel, this feels like a big, bad sin. Hiding you was one thing, but what you're asking me to do now. . . !!

11

(She exits, shaking her head with misgivings. The brass band is now playing away vigorously in the distance.)

PAVEL: *(With the slippers)* Oh, Mama! These did it. It's all wrong, I know, because you made them with such love for your little Pavel, but if you could see what they have done to him, you would rise from your grave and curse the day you stitched them together. *(A helpless gesture.)* It all seemed so simple at first! They gave me a uniform and a gun, taught me how to salute and then on a fine spring day, I kissed Praskovya goodbye and marched off with the others to win the war. And the thought of these *(the slippers)*, waiting for me at home, kept me going . . . kept me smiling and whistling away even when the marches were forced and long. At first the others teased me about them. But as the weeks passed and we tramped further and further away from home, they eventually stopped laughing. The time came, when sitting around at night with no songs left to sing or jokes to tell, sooner or later one of them would say in a small voice: 'Hey, Pavel, tell us about your slippers.' The men would stare into the fire with sad, homesick eyes while I talked about them, about slipping my feet into their cosy padded comfort and settling down next to the stove with Praskovya, to talk about the weather or the pigs or the latest village gossip . . . the silly unimportant little things that break a big man's heart when he is far away from home.

That first winter wasn't too bad. 'Next spring,' we said, trying to cheer each other up, 'we'll be back home next spring.' We even managed somehow to get through the second one with our spirits still intact. But a year later, there we were, once again, watching the first snow fall, and our victorious march back home seemed even further away than ever. And what a winter that one turned out to be, Mama! The oldest among us could not remember snow that deep or temperatures that low . . . winds so sharp and cold the skin blistered and cracked open to the bone. Our hands could barely hold the pitiful crusts of bread we were given as rations. And for what? Why were we all dying of hunger and cold when we had warm homes and young wives waiting for us? The stupidity of it all made me want to vomit up food I didn't have in my belly. That is when they (*the slippers*) lost their innocence and began to torment me. Sitting there huddled in the trench, an image of them would come floating into my deranged mind . . . and with them, smells and sounds . . . of pine logs cracking and hissing away in the stove . . . crusty warm bread and freshly churned butter . . . Weak as I was, I might still have been able to cope with that, but then the little voice started whispering. 'Go home, Pavel Ivanovich, go home.' I tried to shut my ears to it with prayers and patriotic songs, but nothing helped. It just carried on . . . laughing at me and my faltering loyalty, mocking all that was sacred . . . 'There are no flags in either heaven or hell, no causes beyond the grave.' And always the same refrain. 'Go home, Pavel Ivanovich, your slippers are waiting for you. Go home!'

(*In the distance the brass band and voices singing.*)

Am I such a terrible sinner, Mama, for having yielded to temptation under those circumstances . . . half crazed as I was with hunger and cold? One night . . . all I wanted was one more night beside the stove in these slippers, and then I would have happily laid down my life defending our Motherland. But when I came to my senses in here, Praskovya told me that a month had already passed. One day, one week, one month. . . ! It would have all come to the same thing in the end . . . one bullet in the back of the head.

(*An excited and happy* PRASKOVYA *bursts into the sty. She is now dressed in black and carries her Bible and a small Russian flag.*)

PRASKOVYA: Pasha . . . Pasha . . . It's all right, Pasha. It's all over and it's all right. Do you want to hear about it, Pavel?

(*He stares at her in silence. She produces a little black box.*)

To start with, you've been awarded a medal . . . for making the Supreme Sacrifice . . . (*The inscription on the*

medal) 'Pavel Ivanovich Navrotsky. A Hero of the People.'
Your mother would have been so proud. Your name is
also inscribed on the monument. As for Comrade
Secretary Chomski's speech . . . You did the right thing
after all, Pavel, in not going out there. You would have
had a hard time making an appearance after what he had
to say. He started off by urging all of us . . . 'sons and
daughters of our Glorious Revolution' . . . to take a lesson
in self-sacrifice and dedication to the Cause from the noble
comrades whose names have been chiselled in granite for
all future generations to read. The world we live in is safe,
Pavel, thanks to the likes of you . . . 'the Russian bears
who mauled the fascist mongrels' . . . our children, and
their children, and their children's children, will grow up
in a world of plenty for all, thanks to the likes of you . . .
the brave fifty of Sarazhentsy who sacrificed their lives
defending the Revolution in the Winter Campaign of '43.
And finally, the fact that you lie somewhere in an
unmarked grave doesn't really matter, because your
memory is enshrined forever in the hearts of the People.
(*She pins the medal to* PAVEL's *chest.*)
As for our comrades out there . . . a sight to behold! They
wept for you, Pavel, as if you were their very own flesh
and blood. When I returned to my place after laying my
flowers, I thought I was going to end up bruised all over
from the embraces I got for 'our beloved Pavel Ivanovich'.
I'm not exaggerating. That old skinflint Smetalov . . . he
buried his bald head in those money-grabbing paws of his
and wept! All of them . . . Tamara, Galina, Nastasia . . .
every single one of them had the chance for a really good
cry thanks to you. There would have been a lot of
disappointed people out there if you had cut short that
grief with an unexpected appearance. But do you want to
know what is strangest of all, Pavel? There was a time out
there when I myself was so overcome with emotion at the
thought of your lonely and bitter death so far away from
home, that I also started to cry! Yes! Under the power of
Comrade Secretary Chomski's words, for some minutes I

myself believed that you were dead. Look! I'm ready to start again. (*Wiping away her tears*) But that still isn't the end of it. I don't mean to upset you, but it will be on my conscience unless I tell you. When it was all over, Smetalov insisted on walking back with me, and on the way . . . he proposed to me. At least that is what I think he was doing. 'The joyful vision of my pigs and his cows under the same roof' . . . is how he put it. He said it would be a happy ending to the sad story of the Widow Navrotsky. I couldn't get rid of him! He's coming back next week for an answer. (*She makes the sign of the cross.*) Lord have mercy on us . . . Our souls will surely roast in hell for what we have done today. And if our comrades ever find out, we'll be in for a double dose of it. We have lied to them, Pavel . . . publicly! We have made fools of them and a mockery of the anniversary celebrations. Now they will never forgive us.

PAVEL: How is it possible! Like the pigs, all I do in here is eat, sleep and defecate, yet my burden of guilt grows heavier, and heavier. Instead of being diminished by my suffering, it seems to draw nourishment from it . . . like those mushrooms that flourish and get fat on the filfth in here. Has it finally come to that, Praskovya? Is my soul now nothing more than a pigsty?

PRASKOVYA: That sounds like a theological question, Pavel. I don't think I know enough to take it on.

PAVEL: Does ten years of human misery count for nothing in the Divine Scales of Justice?

PRASKOVYA: I think it would be wiser if I left that one alone as well. These are all matters beyond my simple woman's head. I will leave you to deal with them.
(*She gets up to go.*)

PAVEL: Where are you going?

PRASKOVYA: Get changed and then back to work. Celebrations are over. There are chores waiting for me in the house.

PAVEL: (*Staring at her, dumbfounded*) Just like that?

PRASKOVYA: Just like what?

PAVEL: You are going to walk away from me, leave me in here

15

. . . just like that.

PRASKOVYA: Life goes on, Pavel.

PAVEL: Who's life?

PRASKOVYA: Everybody's, I suppose.

PAVEL: Mine as well?

PRASKOVYA: Yes. I pray to God that it goes on as well.

PAVEL: (*Crude sarcasm*) Thank you very much for that information, Praskovya. So, my life is going to go on! How wonderful! Just think of all the challenging possibilities that lie ahead of me in here. The fact that the pigs will be my only company makes the prospect even more exciting, doesn't it? (*Rubbing his hands together in mock relish*) So what should it be? Something in the line of religion? I'm being serious! Maybe there are souls worth saving inside those little mountains of lard. I'll coax them out. Give them all good Christian names and preach the Gospel. St Pavel of the Pigs! You don't like that? Then what about politics? Yes, that's a possibility as well. This pigsty is a very political situation. In those poor, dumb creatures we might have the last truly underprivileged and exploited working class of the world. I could embrace their cause, become a subversive element and breed rebellion. So that when next you try to lead some poor helpless comrade off to the butcher, you find a small revolution on your hands. Have I overlooked any possibilities? Please say something before you go off to peel potatoes or scrub the floors . . .

PRASKOVYA: The potatoes are already peeled . . . I did that first thing this morning . . . and none of the floors need scrubbing. If you're interested in the truth, Pavel, there is a pile of dirty clothes waiting for me. This is washday. So get ready for it . . . I am going to walk away from you.

PAVEL: Just like that.

PRASKOVYA: Just like that.

(*Exit* PRASKOVYA. PAVEL *alone. The pigs grunting away contentedly.*)

SCENE TWO

Beauty and the Beast

The pigsty. A lot of time has passed. Once again a chorus of pig noises initiates the scene. PAVEL *is slumped in mindless apathy. He is swatting flies with what looks suspiciously like the last remnant of one of his cherished slippers. The other is on one of his feet. After a few minutes of this he sweeps together all the dead flies and counts them. That done, he gets up and goes over to a wall where we now see that his calendar of days has been defaced by a tally of dead flies. The score at the moment: 9,762. He adds 23 to this, bringing the total up to 9,785. A few vacant seconds as he stands scratching himself. His next move is to take up his stick and go around the sty tormenting the pigs . . . a pastime he pursues without either enthusiasm or joy. In the middle of this he stops suddenly and stares in disbelief . . . a butterfly has somehow managed to get into the sty. His mood slowly undergoes a total transformation as he watches it flutter around. He is ravished by its beauty, reminding him as it does of an almost forgotten world of sunlight and flowers, a world he now hasn't seen for many, many years. Suppressed calls for* PRASKOVYA. *He decides to catch the butterfly. A hurried search for something to use as a net . . . he decides on his slipper. He hurries back in search of the butterfly . . . a few seconds of panic when he can't find it . . . ecstatic relief and laughter when he does. He stalks it like a hunter, clambering in and out of pens, but it keeps eluding him. His laughter grows and grows. He stops suddenly.*

PAVEL: (*Addressing himself with disbelief*) What is this? Can it be true? Are you laughing, Pavel Ivanovich? (*Answering himself with conviction*) Yes, good comrade. That is perfectly true. I'm trying to catch a butterfly . . . and I'm laughing. (*Which he does with renewed abandon.*) Praskovya! I'm laughing! (*Back to the butterfly, his slipper ready*) We must get you out of here, my dainty darling. This is no place for a little beauty like you. Where are you? Little fluttering friend, where are you? Please . . . oh, dear God! . . . *please* don't die in here. Let me give

you back to the day outside, to the flowers and the
summer breeze . . . and then in return take, oh, I beg
you! . . . take just one little whisper of my soul with you
into the sunlight. Be my redemption! Ha!!

(*He sees it and freezes . . . it has settled in one of the pens.*
PAVEL *approaches cautiously, ready to pounce. Once again a
sudden stop, his eyes widening with horror at the prospect of
impending disaster.*)

No . . . don't . . . no . . . NO!

(*He is too late. A pig eats the butterfly. He goes berserk with
rage.*)

Murderer! Murderer!!

(*Grabbing a knife, he jumps into the pen and after a furious
struggle kills the pig. Terrible gurgles and death squeals from
the unfortunate animal.* PRASKOVYA *bursts in to find a blood-
stained, sobbing* PAVEL.)

PRASKOVYA: Pavel . . . Pavel. . . !

PAVEL: Too late . . . too late . . .

PRASKOVYA: (*Sees him.*) Oh, my God! What happened? Have
you tried to kill yourself?

(*She examines him frantically.*)

PAVEL: (*Still sobbing*) No . . . no . . .

PRASKOVYA: This isn't your blood?

PAVEL: My soul, Praskovya . . . it's my soul that bleeds.

PRASKOVYA: Well then, there is something else in here
bleeding in the old-fashioned way. (*She follows a trail of
blood back to the pen and sees the dead pig.*) Oh, dear me,
just look at her! Did you do that, Pavel? (*She is very
impressed.*) And all by yourself!

(PRASKOVYA *fetches a bucket of water and a rag and helps
the still distraught* PAVEL *to clean himself.*)

What happened? Come now . . . tell me all about it and
then you'll feel better.

PAVEL: (*Collecting himself*) A butterfly, Praskovya . . . a happy,
harmless little beauty with rusty-red wings . . . remember
them? From our childhood? . . . Skipping among the blue
cornflowers . . .

PRASKOVYA: Oh yes, I remember those!

PAVEL: Well, one of them found its way in here somehow . . .
I was busy chastising the pigs when I suddenly saw it
fluttering around. I thought to myself, 'Oh dear, this is no
place for a little butterfly to be. Let me catch it so that
Praskovya can set it free outside.' Which is what I then
tried to do. But . . . the strangest thing, Praskovya! While
I was chasing it . . . (*A little laugh at the memory*) . . . and
once I nearly had it! . . . while I was chasing it, it was as
if something inside me, something that had been dead for
a long, long time, slowly came back to life again. All sorts
of strange feelings began to stir inside me . . . and the
next thing I knew I was laughing! Can you believe that,
Praskovya? Me laughing! In here!

PRASKOVYA: I wish I'd been here for that.

PAVEL: I called you.

PRASKOVYA: I remember that laugh very well. Such a good one
it was! But how do we end up with a dead pig?

PAVEL: I'm coming to that. Don't interrupt me.

PRASKOVYA: I'm sorry.

PAVEL: The little butterfly . . .

PRASKOVYA: Yes.

PAVEL: I was chasing it and laughing . . . the way I used to
when I was a little boy. A moment of magic, Praskovya!
. . . as if it had found . . . in here! . . . a mysterious path
back to my childhood . . . back to the meadows where I
used to romp and play, with flowers and birdsong all
around me, a blue wind-swept sky overhead . . .

PRASKOVYA: That is very beautiful, Pavel.

PAVEL: Oh, yes. So there we were: the butterfly and the little
boy . . . Beauty and Innocence! (*Pause.*) It settled in that
pen.

PRASKOVYA: (*At last she understands*) Oh dear dear dear . . .

PAVEL: (*Nodding*) Beauty and Innocence were joined by the
Beast. (*For a few seconds his emotions again leave him at a
loss for words.*) It was horrible, Praskovya. I saw it coming
but there was nothing I could do to stop it. First the mean
black little eyes focused, the bristles on its snout started
quivering in anticipation . . . but before I could move a

muscle it had opened its loathsome mouth and that was the end of it.

PRASKOVYA: Don't take it too much to heart, Pavel. You tried your best, and God will bless you for your efforts.

PAVEL: God will do nothing of the sort. God doesn't give a damn about what goes on in here.

PRASKOVYA: (*Not sure she has heard correctly*) Pavel?

PAVEL: And if he does, there is nothing he can do about it.

PRASKOVYA: (*Deeply shocked*) What are you saying, Pavel Ivanovich!

PAVEL: I'm saying that God has no jurisdiction in here. And do you know why? Because this is hell! Yes! I know where I am now. I at last know this place for what it really is. Hell! The realm of the damned. *This* is my punishment, Praskovya . . . to watch brutes devour Beauty and then fart . . . to watch them gobble down Innocence and turn it into shit . . . (*Breaking down once again*) And it is more than I can endure. I'm reaching the end, Praskovya. Those few seconds of innocent laughter might well have been the death rattle of my soul.

PRASKOVYA: Come now, Pavel, I know you are very upset but don't exaggerate. You can't have it both ways.

PAVEL: What do you mean?

PRASKOVYA: You can't be both dying *and* in hell.

PAVEL: Why not?

PRASKOVYA: Because any little child will tell you that hell is where you will go *after* you're dead.

PAVEL: (*Nearly speechless with outrage*) You are going to split hairs with me at a time like this?

PRASKOVYA: Just thought you might be interested in the truth, Pavel.

PAVEL: Well, I'm not! Because what you call 'The Truth' invariably involves the reduction of profound philosophic and moral issues to the level of your domestic triviality.

PRASKOVYA: All right, all right, have it your own way. But at the risk of making you even more angry, Pavel, I think I should also point out that only last week I had to let out your trouser seams because you're putting on a little weight around the waist . . . and now you've just killed a full-grown pig with your bare hands. That doesn't sound like a dying man to me.

PAVEL: I meant it *spiritually*! *Inside*! Didn't you hear me? I was talking about my *soul*.

PRASKOVYA: Oh, I see . . .

PAVEL: No, you don't! You see nothing. The full tragic significance of what is happening in here is beyond your comprehension. (*To the wall, with its tally of dead flies*) Look! Look at what I've become! Look at what my life has been reduced to. Nine thousand seven hundred and eighty-five dead flies! The days of my one and only life on this earth are passing, while I sit in mindless imbecility at that table swatting flies. And when I get bored with that, what is my other soul-uplifting diversion? Tormenting the pigs. *They* are now a higher form of life than me. That's the truth! They have at least got a purpose. Crude as it may be, pork sausages and bacon does give their lives a meaning . . . which is more than can be said of mine. I'm not deluding myself, am I, Praskovya? I wasn't always like this. The man you married . . . he was like other men, wasn't he? . . . decent and hard-working with dreams and plans for a good and useful life. Remember our last night together before I went off to the war . . . how we sat up in bed and talked about the future and what we were going to do when I came back . . . the plans we had for a family, for more pigs and a bigger and better sty. That was *Me* . . . the same man whose greatest pleasure now is to flatten another fly on the table top. Do you know what his ambition is? A hundred thousand squashed flies. (*Wandering around the sty*) And to think that my greatest fear was that I would lose my mind. (*Hollow laughter.*) That would have been a happy ending compared to what is really in store for me in here. The punishment reserved for me, Praskovya, is to live on in total sobriety and sanity knowing that I am losing my soul, that a day will come when I'll be no better than that brute I killed. And when that has happened, should Beauty chance to cross my path

21

again . . . (*He swats the imaginary butterfly as he did the flies.*) And look at what I'll be using! (*The tattered slipper.*) Do you recognize this? Can you detect any trace of its former delicacy and beauty under the crust of filth that now covers it? My mother's slippers! These were my most cherished possessions. Look at them now. (*Hurls his slippers into one of the pens.*) There . . . let's make a thorough job of it . . . turn them into shit as well. A life with nothing sacred left in it is a soulless existence, Praskovya. It is not a life worth living.

(PRASKOVYA *does not know how to respond. She alternately nods and then shakes her head and in this fashion gets through a respectful silence before again venturing to speak.*)

PRASKOVYA: (*Timidly*) Pavel . . . I don't mean to interrupt but . . . can I ask a question?

(*No response from* PAVEL.)

What immediate effect does all of that have on things . . . and the situation in here . . . What I mean is . . . I don't want to interfere but it is getting on for supper time and well . . . must I go on with it . . . or what?

(*No response from* PAVEL.)

I was making cabbage soup and dumplings.

(*No response.*)

Pavel?

PAVEL: (*Violently*) I heard you!

(*Another pause.*)

PRASKOVYA: Well?

PAVEL: (*It is not easy for him.*) Have we got a little aniseed for the dumplings?

PRASKOVYA: Yes.

PAVEL: Soup and dumplings.

The Midnight Walk

*The pigsty. A lot more time has passed. There is yet another layer
of graffiti on the walls, consisting this time of obscenities and rude
drawings of the pigs. The animals are in a subdued mood as the
scene starts. It is night. A lit candle on the table.* PAVEL *is on his
bunk, propped up against pillows. He appears to be a very sick
man. Laboured, desperate breathing.* PRASKOVYA *is in attendance.
Laid out in readiness is a woman's outfit . . . dress, shawl, hat and
shoes.*

PAVEL: (*Struggling to speak*) Is it time yet?

PRASKOVYA: Just a little longer.

PAVEL: You said that at least an hour ago.

PRASKOVYA: There are still a few lights on in the street. It
won't be safe until they are all out. Be patient.

PAVEL: 'Be patient'! I'm dying . . . of suffocation . . . and she
says, 'Be patient'!

PRASKOVYA: Shall I keep fanning you?

PAVEL: Useless! All that does . . . is circulate . . . the stench
. . . and foul air in here. I need fresh air . . . fresh air . . .
fresh air . . .

PRASKOVYA: And you are going to get it. Just hang on a few
minutes more. It won't be long now before the village will
be in bed and fast asleep and then we can take our chance
. . . (*Makes the sign of the cross.*) And my God help us. Let
me say once again, Pavel, that I'm feeling more than just a
little nervous. You've had some strange ideas in here, but
this one . . . If it wasn't for your condition I would never
have agreed to it. So remember your promise . . . no
arguments when we get out there. You don't know your
way around any more so *I'm* leading the way, and we're
going as far as the big poplar and then coming back. If
you are up to it and it looks safe, we can maybe think
about a more roundabout route for our return. But that's
all. Agreed?

(*She sees that* PAVEL *is crying.*)

Now what's the matter? Really, Pavel, you spend half your time in tears these days.

PAVEL: Give me your hand . . . feel my heart.

PRASKOVYA: Oh my word yes! What's that all about, Pavel?

PAVEL: Fear. I'm frightened.

PRASKOVYA: Then shouldn't we abandon this crazy idea?

PAVEL: No . . . no . . . it's not just *that*. Everything! My whole life. For all of his fifty-one years, Pavel Ivanovich Navrotsky has been a frightened man . . . and I'm so tired of it now, Praskovya . . . tired . . . tired . . .

PRASKOVYA: Don't aggravate your condition with morbid thoughts. Try to look on the bright side of things.

PAVEL: No, I *must* speak. There are things about me that I've kept hidden, unconfessed truths, that choke me tonight as much as the fetid air in here.

PRASKOVYA: All right, Pavel. *I'm* listening.

PAVEL: (*Sitting up*) I'm a coward, Praskovya! Please, no denials . . . I've got to say it. Pavel Ivanovich Navrotsky is a coward. It's true, Praskovya. Where other men are motivated by patriotism, or ambition . . . I have been driven by fear. The other night, knowing that my end is now near, I tried to remember my childhood, tried to recall for the last time just a few images of those carefree, happy years of innocence . . . but do you know what were the only memories were that came to me? Frightened little Pavel hiding away from trouble! From big bullies looking for a fight, or my angry father with his belt in his hand . . . hiding away under my bed, in the cupboard under the stairs, in the cellar, in the shed at the bottom of the garden. I had a secret little book in which I kept a list of all the places I had found to hide. I believed that if I could find a hundred small, dark little places into which I could crawl and lie very still and where no one would find me, then I would be safe all my life. I only got as far as sixty-seven. And it didn't end in my childhood, Praskovya. As I grew up I refined the art of hiding away. I ended up being able to do it even when I was in the middle of a crowd of people! Like our wedding. I've got a terrible confession to make, Praskovya, you married my black suit. I was hiding away inside it at the time. Or that 'brave' soldier who waved goodbye to you when he marched off to the war. The only brave thing about him was his uniform. I was hiding away inside that one as well. My courage lasted for as long as those buttons were bright. And how does it all end? In a pigsty! And guess what Pavel Navrotsky is doing in the pigsty? This is number sixty-eight.

(*He collapses back on his pillows.*)

PRASKOVYA: There, you've got it off your chest. Do you feel better now?

PAVEL: No . . . if anything I feel worse. If I don't breathe fresh air within the next few minutes, you'll be hiding me away in my grave before the night is out.

PRASKOVYA: Come now, Pavel . . . none of that! I'll go and check again.

(PRASKOVYA *exits and returns after a few seconds.*)

Yes, we can chance it now. All the lights are out.

(PAVEL, *helped by* PRASKOVYA, *gets to his feet and then struggles into the woman's outfit. A difficult operation because of his condition. At the end of it he is very exhausted and has to support himself by leaning on the table.*)

PAVEL: Mirror.

PRASKOVYA: What?

PAVEL: Mirror!!

(PRASKOVYA *fetches a mirror and holds it up so that* PAVEL *can see himself. He straightens up and studies his reflection.*)

(*Tapping a spot on his chest*) Have you . . . have you got . . . a little brooch or something. . . ?

(PRASKOVYA *exits.* PAVEL *adjusts his outfit while she is gone. She returns with a pretty little box covered with seashells in which she keeps her precious things.* PAVEL *rummages through its contents and chooses a brooch.* PRASKOVYA *pins it on the dress.*)

PRASKOVYA: Very good!

PAVEL: Not too loose around the waist?

PRASKOVYA: No. In fact, I think that dress looks better on you than it ever did on me.

PAVEL: Really?

PRASKOVYA: Oh, yes. If it wasn't for your whiskers, I'd
believe that you were the mother or wife of some good
family. Just keep your face covered and say nothing and
nobody will be any the wiser. But don't get carried away.
If we do meet somebody out there or get stopped or
whatever, *I'll* do the talking. The story is that you are my
cousin, Dunyasha, from Yakutsk, and she's as deaf as a
doornail, 'so don't waste your breath talking to her. She
can't hear a thing.' Ready? (*Makes the sign of the cross.*)
Say a quiet prayer that there are no hooligans prowling
around ready to take advantage of two helpless women.
(*They sneak out into the night. The assault on* PAVEL's *senses
is total . . . a gentle breeze, the smell of the earth, stars in the
sky, crickets and the distant barking of a dog. It is more than
he can cope with. After a few deep breaths of freedom, he reels
giddily.*)
Mother of God, what's happening? Pavel? Is this a stroke?
Please don't die on me out here!

PAVEL: The air, Praskovya . . . the fresh air . . . it's making
me drunk . . . hold me . . . hold me up, I think I'm going
to faint . . .

PRASKOVYA: That settles it! Back into the sty! Come, Pavel,
while you're still on your legs. The whole idea is madness.
I should never have agreed to it.

PAVEL: No no no . . . it's passing . . . I'll be all right.
(*A low soft moan of ecstasy escapes from his lips.*)

PRASKOVYA: Not so loud!

PAVEL: Stars, Praskovya . . . stars . . . Look!

PRASKOVYA: Yes, I can see them! But for God's sake keep
your voice down. At this rate we'll have the whole village
awake before we've even started.

PAVEL: And the little crickets! Listen! This is not a dream, is
it, Praskovya?

PRASKOVYA: No, it isn't, but God knows I wish it was.

PAVEL: Just another dream to torment me when I wake up and
find myself back in that shithouse. Pinch me, Praskovya.

26

Come on, pinch me.

(*She does so.*)

Ouch! Oh yes, I felt that! So then it's true. I'm awake and all of this beauty, this soul-ravishing beauty is real! Mother Earth . . . I give myself to you.

(*Opening his arms as if to embrace all of creation, he lurches off into the night.* PRASKOVYA *follows frantically.*)

PRASKOVYA: You're going the wrong way! Left . . . Pavel . . . Dunyasha . . . turn left . . .

(PAVEL *arrives at the big poplar. A few seconds later he is joined by* PRASKOVYA, *exhausted and breathless from trying to keep up with him.*)

In heaven's name stop, Pavel! What's the matter with you? Do you want us to be caught? We're supposed to look like two sober and sensible women out for a stroll and a breath of fresh air before bed. You've been tearing through the night as if a man was after you. We're lucky nobody came dashing out to defend our virtue. (*Looking around*) Well, anyway, here we are. Let's rest a few minutes and get our breath, and enjoy ourselves, then we can make our way back. But for the sake of my poor old legs, let's take it easy this time.

(PAVEL *is sniffing the air like a hungry dog.*)

Yes, wild roses! They've put on quite a show this year. Masses of them everywhere!

PAVEL: (*Still delirious with freedom*) This is wicked.

PRASKOVYA: What have you done now?

PAVEL: This star-studded, rose-scented magnificence! I have no moral right to it, Praskovya. My sins have made me an outcast on this earth, like Adam thrown out of Eden . . . but here I am trying to sneak back past the Guardian Angel for one last little taste of Paradise.

PRASKOVYA: Don't worry about it too much. It looks as if the Almighty had decided to turn a blind eye on what we're up to otherwise we would have been struck down long ago. And it's not as if we're going to make a habit of it . . . I hope.

PAVEL: You know, Praskovya, I thought that in that sty I had

27

become some sort of moral degenerate, that my soul had rotted away in the ocean of pigshit and piss I've been swimming in since God alone knows when. But that is not true! I still have it!

PRASKOVYA: Moderate your language, Pavel. That is not the way a good woman talks.

PAVEL: Oh, most definitely . . . I feel it tonight . . . I feel it stirring!

PRASKOVYA: All right, I believe you. But now that you know you've still got it, don't let it stir you up too much. You're making me nervous, Pasha.

PAVEL: I can't help myself. That little breeze wafting the scent of roses this way is at work on my emotions as if it were a hurricane. I am aroused! I have urges!

PRASKOVYA: God help us. I saw it coming.

PAVEL: Strange and powerful urges!

PRASKOVYA: Urges to do what, Pavel?

PAVEL: That road! That road stretching before us, Praskovya . . . it beckons!

PRASKOVYA: (*Firmly*) No.

PAVEL: Yes! Let's keep walking.

PRASKOVYA: (*Even more firmly*) And I say no! This is as far as we go. We haven't got enough time left, Pavel, 'specially if we're going to take it easy going back. These summer nights are very short. It won't be long now before the sparrows start chirping and we see a little light in the east.

PAVEL: No no no no . . . you don't understand. I'm not talking about adding just a few miserable minutes to this stolen little outing. I'm saying: Let's follow that road into the Future!

PRASKOVYA: To where? It leads to Barabinsk, Pavel.

PAVEL: All right! So it's to Barabinsk we go . . . and then beyond! The Future, Praskovya. A New Life.

PRASKOVYA: What are you suggesting, Pavel?

PAVEL: Escape.

PRASKOVYA: You mean. . . ?

PAVEL: Yes, that's right . . . the unmentionable . . . the unthinkable . . . Escape! What's the matter with you,

28

Praskovya! Have you been so brainwashed that you've forgotten what the word means?

PRASKOVYA: But what about the house, Pavel . . . all our things . . . the pigs. . . ?

PAVEL: Turn our back on the lot and walk away. Yes! Abandon everything. There must be no going back. If we go back, we'll never do it.

PRASKOVYA: So we must set off, just as we are.

PAVEL: Yes. Here and now!

PRASKOVYA: You dressed as a woman, not a rouble in our pockets. . . !

PAVEL: We'll live like gypsies.

PRASKOVYA: You don't know anything about gypsies, Pavel! You've gone mad tonight. I'm not listening to you any more.

PAVEL: If I have, it's a divine madness because it has given me a vision of my Freedom. Yes, Praskovya! I'd rather die in a ditch beside that road, under the stars with a clean wind in my hair, than return to that sty and die of suffocation from pig fart.

PRASKOVYA: Pavel, please calm down and listen to me. If you take to that road and go on walking, you won't die in a ditch with the stars and the wind and all the rest of it. You'll end up in gaol or in front of a firing squad. Come to your senses, Pavel! Look at you. You'll never get away with it in broad daylight. Your splendid 'future' will last as long as it takes to walk to the next village where the police will nab you. Come now, Pasha . . . we're too old for all these grand ideas. Let's just turn around quietly and go home.

PAVEL: Home? Don't use that word! I don't know what it means any more. Waiting for me back there is a foul dungeon which I share with a dozen other uncouth inmates. No . . . no . . . no . . . I've got this far . . . I'm not going back.

PRASKOVYA: (Giving up) OK, Pavel, I've tried my best. If that's the way you want it, go ahead, take to the road and walk. Believe me I will pray very hard that you find your

29

'freedom' and enjoy a long and happy 'future'.

PAVEL: What do you mean? Aren't you coming?

PRASKOVYA: No, you walk alone. I've had enough. This is as far as I go.

PAVEL: You can't just abandon me, Praskovya.

PRASKOVYA: You've got it the wrong way around, Pavel. *You* are abandoning *me*. *You're* the one who is leaving. What are you waiting for?

PAVEL: You seem to be in a hurry to get rid of me, Praskovya.

PRASKOVYA: It's just that I want to get home while it's still dark, but I also feel I should at least wave goodbye to you when you set off.

PAVEL: All right, all right . . . I'm going. (*Adjusting his dress*) So then, this is it. Goodbye, Praskovya.

PRASKOVYA: Goodbye, Pavel.

(PAVEL *takes a few uncertain steps along the road.*

PRASKOVYA *waves.* PAVEL *stops and then returns to her side.*)

PAVEL: Tell you what . . . I'll strike a bargain. If you wait here with me for the sunrise, I'll go back with you. Please, Praskovya! Do you realize how long it has been since I last felt the golden light of a new day . . . saw my shadow on the earth! That's all I ask. It can't be long now surely. Look . . . isn't the sky already turning grey over there?

PRASKOVYA: If it is, then it also won't be long before we find ourselves in very serious trouble. By the time the sun rises half the village is already up and about the day's business. No, Pavel. This is the end of it. It's not that I don't love you, but my nerves can't take any more. After they've arrested you, tell them they'll find me at home.

(*She abandons* PAVEL *at the big poplar and scuttles off back home.*)

PAVEL: Are you leaving me?

PRASKOVYA: (*A voice in the night*) Yes.

PAVEL: You can't!

PRASKOVYA: I have!

(PAVEL, *irresolutely, tries to stand his ground. As the first light of day waxes, his courage wanes. Eventually . . .*)

PAVEL: Praskovya!

(He hurries after PRASKOVYA.*)*

The sty. PRASKOVYA *is waiting.* PAVEL *bursts in . . . a
dishevelled, desperate figure. He has been running and it takes him
a few seconds to get his breath back.*

PAVEL: Your pious soul will rejoice to hear that an Avenging
Angel of the Lord did appear to chase Adam out of Eden.
It took the form of a big, vicious brute with a black
muzzle and long white fangs who came snarling at me out
of the darkness. I've got his teeth marks on my ankle to
prove it. (*Looking around with disbelief*) I don't believe it!
I'm back in here. I was actually out in the world . . . the
world of men and women, trees and flowers, of sunsets
and sunrises . . . it was there in front of me, a road
leading to a new life, but of my own free will, I turned
around and came *running* . . . yes, *running*! . . . back to
this. Oh, God. I was so near escaping. One small burst of
courage! That was all it needed. And if you had given me
a little support and encouragement, Praskovya, I would
have found that courage. A few words would have done it.
'Here's my hand, Pavel. Let's walk.' So what if it had
only lasted a few golden hours? Wouldn't that have been
better than the next eternity of this? But no, here I am
again . . . And why? Because you have finally come to
believe that this is where I belong. My Home! Yes, that
wasn't just an insensitive slip of the tongue out there, was
it!! That *is* what you believe!
(PRASKOVYA *tries to say something.*)
So what does that make me? A pig?
(*Another attempt from* PRASKOVYA *to speak.*)
Some sort of superior pig that God has endowed with
language and rational thought? Your favourite, your pet
pig who you favour with bowls of cabbage soup and
dumplings while the others get hogwash. Is that how you
see me now?
(PAVEL *leaves* PRASKOVYA, *wanders around the sty and then
steadies himself for a final declaration.*)
For thirty years I have tried to hang on to my manhood in

31

here, tried to defend my dignity against assaults on every front . . . body, mind and soul. Your betrayal is the last straw. I am broken. These are the last words that you will ever hear from me. I abandon my humanity! From now on, Praskovya, feed me at the trough with the others.

(*He tears off his clothes and throws himself naked into one of the pens with the pigs. A few seconds of silence while* PRASKOVYA *considers this development. She then gets up and goes over to the pen where* PAVEL *has joined the pigs.*)

PRASKOVYA: I hope you're not being serious, Pavel.

(*No response.*)

Because if you are . . . well . . . I think you might have gone too far this time. This is very insulting, I'll have you know, both to me and to God. I married a man, not a pig, and as far as the Almighty is concerned, I'm sure he'd like me to remind you that you're supposed to be made in His image. So for the sake of everybody concerned, please get out of there.

(*No response.*)

You are provoking me, Pavel. I warn you I might do something we are both going to regret. So for the last time, I beg you. Get out of there.

(PRASKOVYA *kneels and prays.*)

Dear Lord Jesus Christ, I know it's all wrong to be down on my knees praying to you in a pigsty, but I need your understanding and forgiveness at this moment as never before in my life. Dear Lord Jesus, I am being tempted to sin very badly. Feelings I never knew I had have got hold of my soul and are trying to make me do wicked, wicked things. The reason for this urgent prayer, Lord Jesus, is to beg you, to beseech you . . . please *don't* give me the strength to resist temptation. Amen.

(PRASKOVYA *gets up and fetches Pavel's stick. She rolls up her sleeves, kicks off her shoes, tucks her skirt into her bloomers and then climbs into the pen.*)

This is going to hurt me every bit as much as I intend hurting you.

(PAVEL *gets his first whack. A cry of pain.*)

32

Out you get! Come on. Move!
(*Another whack, another cry.* PAVEL *crawls frantically out of the sty.* PRASKOVYA *keeps after him.*)
If you want me to stop . . . *ask* me.
(*Another blow . . . another cry.*)
You better speak to me, Pavel, because I hate to say it, but this isn't hurting me at all.

PAVEL: (*Can't take any more*) Stop! Stop! You're killing me!

PRASKOVYA: Don't worry, I won't go that far. But I would like to hear a few more words.
(*Another whack.*)

PAVEL: Stop it, Praskovya! Have you gone mad?

PRASKOVYA: Now on to your legs.

PAVEL: No. Leave me alone.
(PRASKOVYA *puts all she's got into one final blow.*)
All right! All right!
(*He crawls to his feet.*)

PRASKOVYA: We've done it!

PAVEL: Help me, Praskovya . . . help me!
(PRASKOVYA *fetches a bucket of water and empties it over him.*)

PRASKOVYA: You're on your two legs again, Pavel, and talking. That's as much as I can do for you. Now help yourself . . .
(*She exits.* PAVEL *alone . . . naked, covered in mud and hurting . . . a picture of abject misery.*)

SCENE FOUR

Orders from the Commissar

Night. PAVEL, *still naked and dirty, but now wrapped in one of his blankets. He sits, a lonely, desolate figure in the Stygian gloom of the sty. He is totally exhausted and talking to himself in a desperate effort to stay awake. Pig noises as usual from the darkness.*

PAVEL: Right step, march, left step, march. Comrade Private, head up . . . come on . . . Up! Up! Open your eyes.

(*Responding*) There.

Wide open!

They are.

No, they're not. You're falling asleep again.

Because I am tired for God's sake! I am utterly and totally exhausted.

No no no no, Pavel. If you close your eyes and sleep through another night in here, that will be the end of it.

Then do something. Help me!

I'll tell you a story, Pavel. Are you listening? Once upon a time, in a small village, there was a very very stupid man who woke up one morning and decided that he wanted to be a pig.

Oh shut up!

Don't you want to hear the rest of it? It's got a very funny ending, Pavel. His feet turn into trotters, his nose becomes a snout . . .

I said shut up!

(*Looking around*) I'm awake. Thank God. That was close! OK . . . Back to work. Where were we? Yes . . . we were dealing with the extremely critical situation which has developed in here, and we were . . . going to . . . we were going . . . to . . . we . . . were . . . going . . . to . . .

(*His head falls forward. A few seconds of sleep.*)

PAVEL!!!

(*He snaps awake with terror and guilt.*)

I didn't do it! I didn't do it! I swear I didn't do it!

(*An oily, evil voice*) Naughty . . . naughty! You got away with a few seconds there, didn't you? Very naughty, little Pavel. I think Daddy should take off his belt and drag you out from under the bed and give you a bloody good thrashing!!

(*Abject terror*) I'm sorry, I'm sorry. I won't do it again.

Don't waste our time with promises. We've had them from you before and they've all come to nothing. You know something, Navrotsky . . . you're a total failure . . .

34

and a pathetic one at that! Praskovya was right . . . all you've learnt in here is how to whine and wallow in with self-pity.

(*Nodding encouragement*) Good, good . . . keep it up keep it up . . . Oh, you're finally interested in the truth, are you! Right! You are also a cowardly deserter . . . a traitor to your Motherland . . . And for what? Can you even remember why you betrayed your country and its people? A pair of slippers. (*Heavily sarcastic tone of voice*) A pair of pretty red slippers which dear old Mama made for her darling little Pavel.

DON'T drag my mother into this! Say anything you like about me but *leave my mother alone*!
What do you mean 'leave her alone'! Giving birth to you makes the old bitch an accomplice in all your treachery.

STOP NOW!
(*Pause.*)
WELL done, Pavel. Well done. Brutal and ugly . . . but it worked. Head clear? Oh yes. Crystal clear. Then back to work. No sleep in here until we have found a solution to my now very desperate dilemma. To do that we first need to get to the Root of the Matter, the Root of the Problem. And while we're digging around looking for it, let's keep an eye open at the same time for The Last Straw so that at long last we can get on with it and break the bloody Camel's Back. But hang on now, not so fast! Why waste a perfectly good last straw on imaginary camels when we've got so many fucking real pigs that need to have their backs broken? Now we're getting somewhere. We are going to take that Last Straw and break the back of every fucking pig in here. (*Wild laughter.*) Crack crack crack crack crack crack crack. Bravo! You've done it, Pavel . . . Pavel . . . Pavel . . . Pavel . . .
(*His lunacy spirals away into a voice of quiet and final despair.*)
Pavel . . . Pavel . . . stop now. Leave the pigs alone. And if you can't do that . . . why don't you then just let them go?

35

(*Pause.* PAVEL *floats back slowly out of his delirium.*)

Who said that? Where did that thought come from?
Me.

(*To his mirror*) You said that?
Yes.

Say it again.
Those animals have endured enough abuse from you,
Pavel. Why don't you just let them go now?

Just like that? Just . . .
That's right. Just open the doors, then open the pens and
let them go.
(PAVEL *is left almost speechless by the unexpectedness of the*
idea.)

Unbelievable! So simple . . . so obvious! . . . just let
them go. Yes yes yes . . . of course! It makes total sense.
Just . . . open the doors, open the pens and let them go!

(*Back to his mirror.*)
Then do it, Pavel.

Now?
Yes. Now! What are you waiting for?

All right, all right. Hold your horses while I think about
my pigs. Your suggestion might be simple, but that
doesn't mean it's easy. It involves me ending a relationship
that has survived decades of filth and nonsense and mutual
abuse. I can't just turn my back on it and walk away as if
it all meant nothing.
(*Laughing at himself in disbelief*) My God, Pavel, you're
amazing! You're up to your old tricks, aren't you? You're
stalling for time. Yes, we've caught you at it again . . .
backing away from the moment of decision and action.
Well, it has got to stop! You are going to do it and you are
going to do it now. Open the doors, open the pens and let
them go. That's an order.

All right. All right.
(*A terrified* PAVEL *obeys orders. His first move is to throw*
open the doors to the outside world. He then goes around the
pens, waking up the pigs.)

Wake up! Wake up! (*Kicking and rattling boards*) Come

on! It's all over. Your hour of liberation has come. The Commissar has ordered your immediate and unconditional release.

(*Pig noises increase in volume and agitation as the animals stir into life.*)

All of you . . . onto your trotters . . . Can't you smell it? Freedom! Now out . . . out . . . out . . .

(PAVEL *opens the pens. The pandemonium rises to a powerful climax as the animals stampede out of the sty.* PRASKOVYA *appears. Nightgown and lamp. She sees the open door, the empty pens and realizes what* PAVEL *has done. The sound of liberated, squealing pigs recedes in the distance. A few stunned seconds as the two of them listen to the virginal silence in the sty.* PRASKOVYA *sits down next to* PAVEL.)

PRASKOVYA: (*Whisper*) It's like being in church, isn't it? You feel you've got to say everything in a whisper . . . and think only good thoughts. And so . . . suddenly so calm. And peaceful. My word, Pavel, this is very hard to believe, you know. I never thought it could ever feel like this in here. All the years and years of shouting and violence . . . just gone! (*Shaking her head*) No. This has got to be a dream.

PAVEL: You're awake, Praskovya.

PRASKOVYA: It's really all over?

PAVEL: Yes.

PRASKOVYA: How did you do it?

PAVEL: I obeyed orders.

PRASKOVYA: What do you mean? Orders from who?

PAVEL: (*Pointing to the mirror*) Him. 'The Commissar'! Don't ask me where he came from or what he was doing in here. A good soldier, which I never was, doesn't ask questions. He just obeys orders. They were very simple. 'Open the doors, open the pens and let them go.'

PRASKOVYA: Just like that.

PAVEL: Just like that.

PRASKOVYA: (*Suppressed laugh but still whispering*) I think there's something wrong with me. You've just chased our livelihood out into the night . . . our only source of

37

income . . . our one and only security . . . we sit here on the brink of ruin and all I want to do is laugh. What about you?

PAVEL: I feel nothing.

PRASKOVYA: Well, I'm sorry, but I can't help it . . . I want to laugh.

PAVEL: Go ahead.

PRASKOVYA: You don't laugh in church, Pavel!

(*But she does so all the same.* PRASKOVYA *has a long, side-splitting silent laugh at themselves and their ruination . . . gestures to the open doors, the empty pens, themselves . . . 'All is kaput' . . . etc. etc. Her laugh is infectious. Exhausted as he is,* PAVEL *manages a faint flicker of a response.*)

And now I want to cry.

PAVEL: Go ahead. You're allowed to do that in church, aren't you?

PRASKOVYA: Oh, yes . . . and as loud as you like. (*Wiping her eyes*) Oh, Pavel, I'm so proud of you! I would never have had the imagination or the courage to do it.

PAVEL: Imagination? Courage? Who are you talking about, Praskovya?

PRASKOVYA: You.

PAVEL: (*Shaking his head*) It wasn't like that at all. It was exhaustion that did it. Total and final mental, physical and spiritual exhaustion. I *had* to do something, and that was all I could think of.

PRASKOVYA: This is no time for modesty, Pavel. With that one bold move you have freed us. Let me confess to you now that I had finally given up all hope of us ever escaping from it. I had come to believe that only death would end our misery . . . and I was more than ready for mine. In fact, if you're interested in the truth, Pavel, I was down on my knees telling the Good Lord as much when I heard the commotion down here. But instead, here we sit like two ordinary people with nothing better to do. I don't know about you, but I feel a little light-headed and silly . . . silly enough in fact to want to sing a little song . . .

PAVEL: A song! That's right! People . . . sing, don't they?

PRASKOVYA: When they're happy, but sometimes also when they're sad. Mine would have been a happy song.

PAVEL: Do you still know one?

PRASKOVYA: I think so.

(*She sings a little happy song.*)

So what is the next bold move, Pavel?

PAVEL: (*The open doors.*) Isn't it obvious?

PRASKOVYA: You're going out there again?

PAVEL: (*Nods.*) But I won't hide away in your dress this time. I'm going out there as myself. (*A helpless gesture.*) I didn't know it was coming. I thought I was just getting rid of the pigs so that I could have a little peace and quiet in here. I wanted to close my eyes and sleep more than I've wanted anything in my whole life. But when they started stampeding through those doors to their freedom. . . !!! God, Praskovya, it was epic! The stuff of history. I wanted to join them. If I'd had any clothes on I would have led that charge of liberation out into the world.

PRASKOVYA: You are going to surrender to the authorities?

PAVEL: Yes. It's a crooked fate that ties up a man's freedom and his surrender in the same bundle, but I've got no choice. (*The weak and desperate little smile of the faint-hearted.*) I think it's another order . . . to go out there and face judgment and take my punishment. It's been a long loneliness in here. I've forgotten what it means, what it feels like to look into another man's eyes . . . or to be looked at by them. I'm still frightened . . . but there is something else now as well and it's bigger than my fear . . . I'm homesick, Praskovya, for other men and women. I don't belong in here. Even if my punishment turns out to be a firing squad . . . those men, looking at me down the barrels of their guns, will be 'home' in a way this sty could never have been.

PRASKOVYA: So then let's do it. I'll get you something to wear. (*Starts to leave and then stops.*) It's a pity we can't take on that walk to Barabinsk. I'm ready for it now.

(*She exits. First faint light of the new day through the open doors.* PAVEL *gets a bucket of water and starts to wash*

39

himself. The graffiti on the walls catches his attention. He takes a rag and tries to clean it off. Too exhausted to do a thorough job. PRASKOVYA *comes back with Pavel's black wedding suit. She has changed out of her nightgown.*)

PAVEL: What do you have there?

PRASKOVYA: Don't you recognize it? Your wedding suit.

PAVEL: My God. That goes back a few years. Is it still wearable?

PRASKOVYA: Oh, yes. After all that drama we had about your uniform, I've made a point of looking after this very carefully. I had a feeling you might need it again one day.
(PAVEL *starts to change into the suit.*)
How are we going to do it, Pavel? There aren't any anniversary celebrations on the go this time. I don't think it will work to just stand on a street corner and announce to the world who you are and what you've done. I'm not sure anybody will bother to listen to you. There are all sorts of loonies around these days and nobody pays them any attention except the police. Maybe that's your best idea, the police station.

PAVEL: (*Offended*) I'm not just a common criminal, Praskovya. As I remember it, the *Military Manual* listed desertion as one of the most serious offences a soldier could commit. I'll hand myself over at the military barracks.
(*He is now dressed.*)
Come . . . let's go.

PRASKOVYA: If it's any consolation, I think we're in time for the sunrise you missed yesterday.
(*They leave the sty.*)